THE MAN'S HANDBOOK FOR CHOOSING THE RIGHT WOMAN

THE MAN'S HANDBOOK FOR CHOOSING THE RIGHT WOMAN

*Understanding Our Relationship Rosters &
What Makes Men Afraid of Settling Down*

By

JACK A. DANIELS

Mill City Press
Minneapolis, MN

Mill City Press, Inc.
212 3rd Avenue North, Suite 570
Minneapolis, MN 55401
612.455.2294
www.millcitypublishing.com

ISBN - 978-1-934937-53-2
ISBN - 1-934937-53-3
LCCN - 2008942840

Cover Design and Typeset by Sophie Chi

Printed in the United States of America

DEDICATION

*This book is dedicated with great love and
gratitude to my family and many friends who
pushed me to pursue my passions and purpose.*

TABLE OF CONTENTS

INTRODUCTION

Throughout this book I will attempt to challenge you to take the time to pause and truly examine yourself without any predispositions, prejudices or false perceptions that inhibit your ability to vividly voice your truths. It is my hope that some of the tools given and discussed will aid your efforts in planting the foundational seeds of success that assist you in truly harnessing the power to maximize your full passion, potential and purpose. I hope that those implanted seeds will then blossom into a strong foundation of faith that continuously fosters your growth and development in an effort to overcome any and all of the mitigating circumstances or situations that you have been allowing to systematically and psychologically sabotage your happiness and success as it pertains to relationships. I am hopeful that some of the discussed strategies and stories will motivate and inspire you to implement, institute and initiate the changes in your life that turn your pride into prayers, pains into purpose and your fears into faith. Moreover, this book will attempt to help you better understand what it takes to start, stabilize and sustain a healthy, happy, lasting, committed relationship you've been so desperately seeking.

In addition, I will attempt to dispel any discrepancies that exist between men and women in an effort to rationalize, reconnect and reposition us to build healthy sustainable relationships that revitalize the institution of family within the context of our collective culture. Of course many of you are reading this and are hoping to receive the inside scoop as to how men actually think. I can respect that and I'm certain you'll actually get several take away points from this interaction. Thanks for the love and support! Enjoy…

"Keep the faith, keep making it happen and remember to stay out of your own way!"

Jack A. Daniels

CHAPTER ONE

COACHES STRATEGY MEETING

"Hard work doesn't come without sacrifice."

I'm savvy, successful, straight, black and single? Now according to every standard and statistic this dilemma should in no way be occurring, but my reality and the reality of several other men displays another truth. Believe it or not, there are several men who value and desire to be in healthy, loving and committed relationships with women. The dichotomy of this dilemma is the disconnection that's occurring with the process it takes for men to better understand how to secure the relationship they so desperately seek.

Trust me I get it, there are some things that were never explained to me in this journey throughout manhood either. Sure my father sat me down and told me the truth about the birds and the bees, but unfortunately, his synopsis was stale, unrehearsed and lacked everything in between that led up to the sex. Truthfully, I'm not even certain we would have had the conversation if my mother wasn't pregnant with my kid sister at the time. I was eight years old and really didn't remember much of anything other than, "You have a penis and the girl has a vagina." "Having sex makes babies...Make sure you don't bring any babies up in this house; you hear me boy?" Despite the fact I was only eight years old and probably couldn't produce any parts of sperm yet, that was pretty much the extent of my man to man talk about women. So naturally, the rest of my vast knowledge came from none other than multiple insecure inexperienced adolescents that most folks refer to as their friends. (sigh)

Fast-forward to present day and unfortunately you'll probably find several men who have yet to unveil the truth about what it takes to search for, start, stabilize and sustain a healthy lasting relationship. Don't worry, it's not your fault. The gap of garnering this revelation has more than likely been a mystery to you for awhile now. In fact, I've compiled a list of questions that you've probably asked yourself on more than one occasion.

1. What makes me do the things I do when it comes to relationships?
2. Why does it seem like I keep dating the same woman over and over?
3. Why can't I settle down and be with just one woman?

4. Why can't I find the perfect woman who satisfies all of my wants and needs?

5. I really do want a wife someday, but how do I choose the right woman?!

Personally, I've asked myself these questions a million times over and hope to shed some light on our not so easy to discuss shared dilemma throughout this book. I could easily give you countless selections of psychological case studies and babble, but simply put, the underlining answer to all of the questions asked above is "You." You make the choices to do what you do during the relationships you've experienced. You keep choosing the same woman to date, you make the choices to cheat and you decide when you're ready for the perfect woman to come into your life and satisfy all of your requirements, wants and needs. After discovering her, hopefully "you" will find the courage to ask her to be your wife. Still with me I hope?

This is Going to Take Some Work

A good friend and I were heavily engaged in a conversation about what it would truly take for his woman to satisfy and please him. He simply couldn't understand why and how the process of one woman making him happy was so hard. He was convinced that he had covered all of the bases in the course of their relationship and was at a loss as to what else he could do to remain faithful. According to him, he was unhappy with her inability to satisfy all of his desires. Of course everyone who knows me knows that I'm extremely passionate about invoking thought and challenging the way people process information whenever given the opportunity. Thus, in answer to his dismal disposition and perplexing problem I quoted one of my favorite riddles. "It's more powerful than God, more evil than the devil. Rich people need it and poor people have it. If you eat it, you will surely die." "What am I?" I tend to challenge people with this riddle because I find it amazing at how most of us often make simple solutions into complex concerns.

There's no easy way around it, relationships are hard work. The energy and efforts required in fostering the growth and development of a lasting relationship is even harder. When you factor in the element of dealing with the unpredictable emotional rollercoaster rides women traditionally put us on, you've just multiplied your efforts times twenty-eight! (depending on when her cycle falls) Everyone encounters complications within their relationships. The truth is none of us have had any degree of formalized training on how to truly make them work. We've had formalized training in every other facet of our lives. Science, mathematics, sports, diversity, sex and so on, but not relationships. Furthermore, as men we've been conditioned to constantly search for the woman who we think encompasses all of the elements necessary for making us happy. I'm not going to bore you with a bunch of self analysis case studies and psychiatric babbling. Simply put, being happy requires you doing the work! Abraham Lincoln said, "Most folks are as happy as they make up their minds to be." Most people have the misconception that their happiness comes from other people. It's not her job to make you happy; that accountability belongs to you. In my time of working with couples I've observed that most of the time the person who is the unhappiest in the relationship is often the same one who needs to spend the most time self-examining. Now that's not to say it occurs that way always, but quite often people's exaggerated expectations and perceptions overshadow the truths and realities of their individual situations and circumstances.

Fellas, what can the next woman really give you that your current one can't? Do you think the next one isn't going to bring a totally different set of new issues to the table? Does the thrill of new explorations, expectations and experiences outweigh someone who loves and accepts you for you? The truth is, until you have honestly assessed and dealt with all of the problems of your past, dilemmas you never discussed and the monsters you hide under the multiple masks you wear daily, you will forever be a fugitive forging falsified illusions of faithfulness. Be true to yourself and do the necessary work it takes to make your self whole and happy. If you continue to run from one relationship to the next without pausing to acknowledge and assess what is or has possibly caused the demise of the last one, you're doing nothing but perpetuating the existence of a systemic cycle of selfish, self-indulgent, self-destructive behavior.

Overall, remember that you control your level of happiness. Stop running from yourself and confront your countless complexities. Stop fooling yourself acting as if you're invincible, nothing bothers you and no one has ever hurt you. Until you have acknowledged, discovered and tapped into the true man God has anointed and purposed you to be, you will never be truly satisfied or happy. And in case you were wondering, the answer of what a "woman" needs to do in order to truly satisfy and make you happy is ironically the same answer to the above riddle. (nothing) It's not up to her, it's up to you. You have to man-up, stop running from yourself and do the work!

Strategy Synopsis

To better understand what it takes for you to do the work necessary to getting to a place of understanding yourself and the decisions you make as it pertains to women and relationships, I'm going to break it down to the universal great equalizing language of men. (Sports) Throughout this book I'm going to show how a man defines himself through the women that represent the core components of his character by metaphorically contrasting the similarities to creating and coaching a championship basketball team. As men, until you have explored, experienced and expounded upon all of the components that comprise your character as a man, you will never be ready to fully commit yourself to a relationship. And unless you have all of the components that make up the essence of a championship team, you'll never be ready to take on the competition you'd face on your road to the championship game. With that said, let's just jump right into it.

CHAPTER TWO

POST-SEASON ANALYSIS

"Winners know that failure isn't final;
it's a precursor for progress."

S o everyone knows you have to know where
you've been in order to get to where you want
to be right? If that's the case, assessing prior
year's performances are essential to understanding what
has and hasn't worked. A coach is only as good as the
players on his team, the goals he sets and the strategies
he implements to execute those goals. The past years
have been dismal and unsuccessful in reaching our
goals which is why this coaches meeting is mandatory.
We need to develop a game strategy and a team that
encompasses the necessary elements that foster the
growth and development of a championship caliber team.
It's imperative that we challenge ourselves to carefully
review each potential candidate with scrutiny in an
effort to ensure they represent the components that help

us succeed where we've failed in the past. We've had a losing streak that has crippled our confidence, courage and commitment to winning. So when comparing this synopsis to women, we haven't experienced the essence of a successful sustainable relationship because we have yet to discover all the core components of ourselves that make us whole, ready and available to fully contribute and commit to a successful relationship. To better understand this analogy I'll be comparing and contrasting the events of my prior seasons.

My Prior Years Postseason Analysis

Without boring you with the details, I have no shame in admitting my failure. In fact, it's because of my failures that I consider myself a vessel that can vicariously voice this vision to you now. Like most downward dives, my spiraling was triggered by a traumatic life altering event; I went through a divorce. Unfortunately, there are many people who can relate to this dilemma. You wake up and go through your normal routine and think to yourself, "How did I get here?" This is not how I dreamed it would be. What happened to all the laughter, no arguments, the big bank account, big house, fancy cars, trips to different countries, 2.2 kids, great friends and the dog that everyone knows is a part of the family? That is how it always played out on television, so most of us naturally anticipate our lives to mirror those projected images. I'll be the first to say that when reality hits, it hits hard. And the crumbling reality of my perception of a perfect life slapped me harder than ever. I never in my life thought that I would be in such a dark and desolate place.

So now I considered myself a failure. Truthfully speaking, this was a new concept and experience for me. Sure I had failed at minor tasks, but those tasks could never be considered life altering. They were merely molehills that were part of life's teaching and growing process. I failed when trying to learn how to ride a bike without training wheels the first few times. I failed when I tried to dunk my first basketball, I even failed a few test in my day, but those things paled in comparison to the feeling I had after going through my divorce. Like most people, I thought this was not supposed to happen to me. In my mind I had grown accustomed to telling myself that I was a winner; I didn't know how to lose. Losing was never an option in my mind. Forget about the people who believed in team spirit and the belief that it was never about the winning, it was only about how you played the game. I always considered anyone who thought that way to be a loser who probably never had a chance of winning anyway. I thought they would never amount to anything but failure because they never set their minds on the end result of winning. They were simply happy with just playing whatever game they were participating in. Sure I enjoyed the sport of playing the games, but I also began with the mindset and vision of how I would come out on top and victorious at the end of those games.

Winning felt good and normal to me. So much so that it became a natural expectation in any situation or circumstance that I entered into. I was relatively successful in just about every facet of my life. Not because I deserved to be, but because God had shined on me and truly blessed my walk and way through life. I was the person that faithfully encouraged and educated everyone else about how to seek and secure their personal seasons of success. How could I confidently look the countless people in the eye who looked up to me and looked at my life as an example and motivating map of hope without having shame and embarrassment written all over my face? I had given so many other people and couples counseling strategies that assisted them in turning their stumbling blocks into stepping stones of success. Now look at me; I was a mess. I felt as if I had let so many people down. I had the weight of the world on my shoulders and had no idea on how to shake the feelings of guilt, shame and failure from my mind. Those feelings of helplessness, hopelessness and heartache could have sent me psychologically spiraling towards the dark roads of depression if I didn't get a hold of myself.

The truth is, you can try to plan every step and strategy you ever take throughout life, but there is no guarantee that says your meticulous thought out action plans will come to fruition. Life has a funny way of throwing curve balls at you when you were expecting the fast pitch straight down the middle. You swing and hit nothing but wind as the ball teeters to the outside of the plate where you least anticipated it to be. After you have just about thrown your back out from not making contact with the ball, you limp back to the dugout with embarrassment because you just cost your team the biggest game of the year due to your expectation of how things were supposed to go. You were confident you would connect with that ball because you thought you knew every one of the pitcher's tricks. You were wrong and never saw his curve ball coming. The moment that was supposed to end with the team hurling you up on their shoulders and carrying you off of the field ended up totally opposite than the way you dreamed it up. You lost and the season is over.

Like most life altering circumstances and situations, I can attest that my failed marriage could be considered the makeshift moment that mentally crippled my courage, confidence, conviction and character. After that blow, I was temporarily not the same man I used to be; I was a little shorter than people were accustomed to seeing me and more broken than the average person. I label my divorce as my 'familiar failure.' Whenever trials, troubles or tribulations impact and affect your life, we often find it difficult to see our way out of that circumstance or situation immediately. However, when the world has knocked you flat on your back and it seems as if no one cares and there is no one around to help give you a helping hand to pull yourself back up, it is those moments we should cherish most because they help to define us.

Despite losing something you hold extremely valuable, there is always room for continued growth and potential to discover something new you had no idea ever existed. I am a firm believer that our dark times are the catalysts that help catapult our potentials and help define our Divine purposes. Which is why restructuring, re-strategizing and repositioning your self for success plays a pivotal role in successfully re-entering into a healthy lasting relationship. So the question is, "How do you pick yourself up, rebuild and reposition yourself to take on the competition of forgetting about your failures?" You focus on what good looks like to you and what it will be like once you get back to being the champion everyone knows and loves which is the process I'm going to communicate to you throughout this book. Changing the success of your season depends on you and the love you have for the game of life! So let's play some ball!

CHAPTER THREE

TRYOUTS

"Everyone that shows up shouldn't be shown in."

Disclaimer: Before we begin and every woman on the planet gets angry for this analogy, let me park here parenthetically to say that not every man goes about discovering himself in the same manner. Furthermore, the making of his team doesn't always occur simultaneously. These scenarios can either play out sporadically, concurrently or simultaneously over the course of his life. Results and scenarios vary on an individual basis.

1ˢᵗ Day of Practice

So today is the first day of practice and its time to pick the players you think are crucial to building a championship caliber team. Tryouts are bigger than simple days of practice. Sure you'll get players of all sorts trying to make it on your team because you're one of the hottest coaches in the league! Trust me, the players trying out have already done their homework. They've heard about your work ethic, how you communicate, collaborate and sacrifice for your players. You have all of the elements they're looking for in a coach that compliment them as players. What they don't know is that your selection process is the beginning of a process that's larger than they as players will ever know.

However, before you begin randomly selecting who you think will be good fits for your team, you need to better understand the rules of engagement and the psychology behind the selection process because this could get very ugly if you're not careful. The process of selecting the players on your team requires a great deal of honesty about who you are and where the players actually stand as it pertains to your team.

*Let me take a sidebar to further explain what I refer to as our sophisticated booty calls.

Sophisticated Booty Calls

There's a couple who has been dating for about two and half years and feels as if everything is going quite well. He claims to love her and she feels the same way. They have a wonderful time whenever they're together and have every intention of doing what it takes to keep each other happy. They both live in different cities 600 miles apart from one another. They only get to see each other maybe once a month, but according to her, they make the best of every moment they do see each other. (how sweet) He really prefers to come and visit her versus her coming to see him because her house is more comfortable. In fact, she finds it to be a very chivalrous gesture and she's only been to see him twice since they've been dating. (sigh) She's ready to take their relationship to the next level and is confused about what's taking so long. He however has expressed to her that he is very hesitant, needs more time and still unsure about wanting to take that next step. He also throws in the occasional lame line of, "I really like things the way they are with us so why do we need to mess up what we have?" (sigh again) I'm almost scared to address this dilemma in fear of having my player's license revoked, but fellas we just have to do better.

In the past, I've received multiple letters from women asking me to address some of the problems and issues men have with fully committing themselves to a woman and it's safe to say that every situation is going to be different than the next. However, as it pertains to the above scenario, it's imperative that we're more honest with ourselves and the women we are with about what the relationship truly means to us. Do you really view yourself having a future with her or is she really just a sophisticated booty call?

Commitment is a big word and often gives us the chills when we mention it in casual conversations. Of course some of the biggest injustices are not the fact we aren't ready to commit or even believe it's fully possible to commit. The biggest injustice comes from the lies we tell that keep women in blatantly biased boxes of bewilderment while we continue to baffle and blind fold their optimism by dangling carrots on our strategy strings of disillusion. While she's dreaming and wishing, you're dodging and wasting time. While she's hoping and praying, you're hopping and preying on everyone else who happens to come your way. So the question is why? Well, the majority of uncommitted men tend to place the women they're dating into categories; the freak, the friend or the forever. (Of course these aren't the categories we'll be utilizing for our team) The freak is our straight up drop-it-like-its-hot no questions asked woman. She's likely to be promiscuous and extremely sexual. She doesn't fit our criteria for a long-term relationship, but we just can't let her go because of...well, you get the point. The friend is perhaps the practical platonic one who we can go to when we feel vulnerable or need advice. We trust her and she helps us somewhat get in touch with our emotional side. She's also the one who gives us pointers on how to continue maintaining the integrity of our stringing strategies. The forever is usually the one who encompasses all three elements. She's the good-girl-wife-material and deserves to be treated with the promise of potential.

When we get all of whatever we claim to be in our system out, we'll settle down, marry her and perhaps have some kids. She's our star player and we treat her like the lady she is. What's problematic is women often have no idea which category they fall into as a result of our stringing strategies. In fact, if you asked most of them, they'd swear they were in the forever category! We lead them to believe they're more than what we know they are and we truly need to do a better job at either revealing our strings or cutting them altogether.

Fellas, we have to do better at respecting ourselves and our women enough to not downgrade their status to nothing more than sophisticated booty calls. It's time to man-up and do the work necessary inside of our hearts and minds so we can stop the confusion of being indecisive, inconsistent and inconsiderate about misleading our women to believe the untruths we tell only to keep them tangled in our webs of misdirection. Trust me I understand playing the field, but be honest about the game you're playing. Commitment is hard and requires a grave sacrifice. Remember that God won't put more on you than you can bear. Be man enough to make the conscious decision to be honest with yourself and the woman you're with about where the relationship truly stands. Is she your freak, your friend or your forever? Whichever one she is, be man enough to let her know where she stands and stop leading her to believe the relationship is more than what you know it is.

Back to 1ˢᵗ Day of Practice

Ok, so you got the honesty part right? It's important to note that while the discussion about categories proves to be very true for some of us, our overall goal will be learning how to better understand the internal components of character we need to explore more meticulously. Essentially, we need a starting five group that is capable of representing every component necessary for us to define ourselves as a winning team. Oh yeah, by the way, throughout this book, please note I will be using the following analogies to help me describe the process of what makes us whole, happy and sometimes afraid of settling down.

- Team = Represents "you" and the components that comprise your character
- Coach = You
- Players = The women you've had, have or will encounter throughout your life
- Game = Life
- Championship = Becoming healthy, whole, happy and ready to fully settle down

So you're single and available. Naturally there's going to be a massive influx of available women trying to demonstrate their skill sets, worthiness, potential and added value to you and your team. What's problematic is that you only have one set of eyes and a limited amount of time so you can't possibly notice and select everyone who's trying out. Truthfully, you already have a great idea of what you're looking for and who will make your roster this year before they even tryout, but you have to go through the process because you never know who just might show up. I can attest to this process very well and I'm elated to share with you some realities of the roster that helped facilitate my road to relationship redemption and readiness.

CHAPTER FOUR

MY 1ˢᵀ DRAFT PICK

"There's no substitute for a solid foundation."

G ood coaches know when you're building a team, it's important to have a solid foundation in which to build that team around. First draft picks are typically the ones that help facilitate this philosophy. Because of the end result of your last relationship, it's statistically proven that most folks tend to return to what they know. It's not rare that after a breakup occurs for an individual to retreat back into the convenience of what's familiar to them. This means old girlfriends, flings and platonic friends are all suspects of sabotaging your future success. You look to them for answers as to why you failed. You hope they can possibly give you some advice or pointers on what you did wrong in the past. You ask, "Was what we had or was I really that bad? If you're just getting out of a relationship I think it's important to proceed with more caution than most. Before you evaluate or choose who your first draft pick will or has been it's important to acknowledge that your "Ex" became your "Ex" for a reason. Because you're vulnerable, hurt and possibly heart broken, you're more prone to pick who and what you're familiar with for your first draft selection. This means you have to be careful to not fall into the trap of repeating and being disillusioned by getting involved in the same type of relationship and repeating the same cycle again.

Your Ex Became Your Ex for a Reason

Let me first say that I really do admire people who take chances when it comes to love. Truthfully, in order to be successful, you have to, but let me put my warning stamp on going backwards. Old flames are typically re-ignited into new flames because we tend to want to believe in the possibility of the fire being different. Last I checked, fire was still made the same way and it's still hot to the touch! The reality for most of us is there was a reason why our ex's became our ex's. Now I'm not naive enough to say people's situations, circumstances or characteristics don't change; they sometimes do for the better. However, more often than not, you'll find that their poots still smell the same, the funny way they eat chicken ain't changed and the same tendency to mistreat you, make you climax, disappoint, degrade and not give you the love you felt like you deserved years ago may possibly be the same also! We try to fool ourselves into believing things will be different the next time around, but we often exit relationships for good rational reasons. The reasons for re-entering those relationships tend to not be as rational as our exit. Have you ever randomly ran into a person you used to date and after talking to them for 5 minutes you're shaking your head, telling yourself silently, "She still looks good, but I can't do it because she still crazy!" Or you try to give a relationship one more chance because you felt like you didn't do everything you could have done to make it work only to discover you really should have listened to your first instincts of moving on. Now you're stuck trying to figure out another exit strategy that's mutually beneficial and won't cause you any bodily harm for leaving again. (whew)

Overall, relationships are hard work and require both parties ready and willing to do the work necessary to foster the growth and development of the relationship. Often times, the balance of old relationships are skewed and unbalanced. One person often feels a stronger connection and commitment to the way things could have, should have and would have been "if." If she never cheated on me, if she didn't have kids, if she cooked a little better, if she didn't talk too much, wasn't so selfish, so sensitive or if she just would have done it the way Keisha does it we might have been ok and so on. The "what ifs" are what typically get us in trouble when considering giving an old relationship another try. I believe in love whole heartedly and encourage everyone to follow their hearts because that's the way God ordained it. However, if you do decide to go down memory lane with an old fling or someone you know had some habits, attitudes, beliefs and expectations that were problematic when you were together the first time, don't go back thinking things have changed that much. Don't be fooled, trust me, the same public representative she sent to hook you the first time is the same one you see this time. Give her time to unmask her true colors and you'll see. The more time you spend with her, the more you're clear about how and why your ex became your ex in the first place! Whatever you do, don't backtrack and get caught up repeating the same cycle.

And My First Selection Is...

Knowing the fact about ex's and how they can get you in trouble led me to build my team around the center position. Playing the position of center on a basketball team is a huge and lonely responsibility. Most centers have been outcast the majority of their lives because of their gargantuan heights. They often try to blend in with normal folks, but frequently fail because it's difficult hiding or playing small when you're that big. More importantly, centers have a unique ability to command attention. Their mobility is somewhat limited, but they have a good sense about the fundamentals of the game. Centers move slower, they're solid like rocks and are good sources of foundation for a team's stability. Furthermore, first draft selections require huge investments and generally need lots of attention because they're new to this level of play. The level of play is heightened and the bars of expectations are raised significantly. Most are young, inexperienced and lack patience and poise, but they have the potential to eventually emerge into superstars if coached correctly.

Lesson #1 – Honesty and Humility

This particular relationship was extremely instrumental to me since it was the first time I'd selected or been with anyone since my divorce. Furthermore, it was the testing ground to ensure if I was ready to be pursuing another championship so soon after the demise of my last attempt. She was everything anyone could hope for. Her characteristics and qualities exceeded every expectation I had for a woman. Honestly, I thought she was too good for me when we first hooked up. She captivated my attention like none of the other women who showed up for tryouts. She was special and had a glow that lit up the room when she walked in. I was drawn to her and knew she'd be mine before we even spoke.

So most people would ask, "If she was all that, why

aren't you still with her?" Good question. Most things in life are about timing and position. And in her case, the timing wasn't right for me to be in the position of a relationship with her. More importantly, the lessons I learned from my first draft pick were honesty and humility.

You have to understand that for the first time in my life I felt like a loser. I was accustomed to winning in every endeavor I chose to undertake. Before I met Michelle I had not been honest with myself about the demise of my divorce, what I was mentally going through and truthfully what I wanted out of life. I was a smooth talking charmer who could sell water to a whale if I so chose. My level of confidence combined with swagger was heightened by every encounter and success I had with women. I was in no way honest or forthcoming about my intentions with whoever I was with because I knew I could string out the best of the best longer than a ball of yarn. However with Michelle, those tendencies came to a screeching halt. The innocence, inexperience and purity she brought to the table revived and rekindled my hope in the essence of women and relationships. She was young, untainted and excited about life and all of its exciting possibilities. I needed that type of spirit to reassure me that the possibility of promise still existed.

Unfortunately, our demise can be attributed to her same hopeful youthful exuberance that manifested itself into the lack of truly understanding my aged experiences. I was too hurt to give her what she deserved and knew it wasn't fair to string her along for the convenience of satisfying whatever pleasures I desired at the time. I was with her because I was afraid of being alone and also acknowleding, confronting and dealing with the hurt I was suffering as a result of the demise of my last relationship. I needed to heal and Michelle provided me with the audacity to be honest and humble about beginning that healing process.

Confrontation is Sometimes a Good Thing

I think it's safe to say that there are many things in our lives' we tend to put off, ignore or simply avoid instead of dealing with or resolving whatever the issues are we're confronted with. What's problematic about this approach of avoidance is that the only way to truly resolve an issue is confrontation. Now I'm not speaking of the confrontation where we find ourselves resorting to violence or physical aggression, I'm speaking of the ability to rationally, respectfully and reasonably resolve matters we tend to be up against. Dealing with problems of our past, dilemmas we never discuss and hiding the monsters under the masks we wear on a daily basis should all be considered culprits of avoidance behaviors. As men, avoidance behaviors are in no way appropriate or healthy. Unfortunately, the more we avoid things rather than confront them, we subject ourselves to feelings that can lead to several addictions and compulsive behaviors. The danger in having the attitude of avoidance is becoming too comfortable with numbing out whatever issue you're confronted with. Alcohol abuse, drug abuse, domestic violence, working longer hours, lying, infidelity and insecurity are all examples of numbing tactics we utilize to avoid confronting our true challenges or issues.

The good news is we all have a choice of whether or not we want to accept or reject the challenge of confrontation. If you're the only person standing between the guy charging at you with the football for a touchdown that's going to win the game, you don't simply step to the side and let him run right in for the score. No, you confront him head on and put him on his back with a tackle he'll never forget! You don't give a guy a wide open shot 4 feet away from the basket when you're standing right there, you contest it by trying to block it. Confronting an issue is very similar to competition. When we play, we typically play to win, but we win by being competitive enough to embrace and confront the challenges of our opponent's opposition toward achieving our goal of winning head on. If we avoided or underestimated our opponent's capabilities by not preparing or not showing up ready to compete on a higher level than them, we'd lose. The same values hold true in any circumstance or situation we find ourselves trying to avoid. Conversations we need to have, tests we need to have performed, relationships we need to end, jobs we need to find, hurts we need to heal, people we need to check or arguments, anxieties and angers we need to resolve. Whatever it is you call yourself avoiding is still going to exist until you confront it and deal with it head on.

Fellas, I know as men we're more apt to avoid a lot of our feelings and thoughts about given situations; we've been conditioned that way. Despite our socialized defects, avoiding whatever circumstances, problems or issues you may have is not the proper way to resolve the problem; confrontation is. Stop running from and start confronting your fears, faults and failures. Confront your insecurities, issues, pressures and problems. Stop avoiding whatever it is that is holding your life hostage. Numbing the pain of reality does just that. After the numbness wears off, you'll still wake up with the same problem you've been trying to avoid by numbing yourself in the first place. Challenge yourself to be man enough to confront your problems head on in order to cease the behaviors associated with avoidance.

In hind sight, you could easily compare Michelle's position of playing center to me shifting, refocusing and *centering* my attention on the work and process I needed to undergo in order to fully heal. From afar, most people would say Michelle played her position very well. Personally, I'd tell you that her presence was pivotal in securing the foundation of my future success. The center is who everyone on the team looks up to in one way or another. Moreover, she was a young, enthusiastic, inexperienced and an excited player who stood out from the crowd and did wonders when it came to helping me and my team rebound. Ironically, "Rebound" would be the same name most people would call her if they were evaluating her significance in my life.

Coaches Evaluation Sheet:

Define who you think you'd select as your 1st Draft Pick and list the qualities you like most about her?

My 1st Draft Pick is _____

The qualities and characteristics I like most about her are:

1. _____
2. _____
3. _____
4. _____
5. _____
6. _____
7. _____
8. _____
9. _____
10. _____

The lesson(s) I'm learning or learned from _____
is: _____

_____

_____

_____

_____

_____

_____

_____

_____

_____

_____

CHAPTER FIVE

THE FRANCHISE VETERAN

*"Experience counts and can consult
you in times of confusion."*

Next up is the veteran. The veteran on a team is the player who has a heightened level of experience. They've been playing in the league for awhile, probably have been on one or more teams before and know what it takes to win. In addition, you don't have to waste your time giving them basic instructions or walking through how the process works; they already know. In fact, most of them know it better than you. Veterans are franchise players who know their position and will play it effectively and efficiently because they understand their value and want nothing more than what's good for the team. They've been at this for awhile and are ready and willing to swallow their egos and pride for the sake of winning. For this reason, veterans can usually be considered consultants in times of confusion. With that said, I picked an older woman to play the position of my veteran shooting guard. She was reliable, consistent and experienced. So when it comes to relationships, I had to ask myself, "Are older women the way to go these days?"

Are Older Women the Way to Go?

One day I was sitting in a sandwich shop having lunch and my attention on the food I was eating was thrown off by a woman who lit up the room and made me do a double take when she walked through the door. Yeah, yeah, yeah, I know what you're saying, "You have weakness for women so what's new about that ?" Well, I'll admit to that, but trust me this one was different. She had long flowing hair, full succulent lips, beautiful smooth chocolate skin that made me want to take a bite out of crime, strong, long legs and was working those heels like she was on America's Next Top Model! Sounds normal right? The difference between her and my regular eye catching show stoppers was about 20 to 25 years! This woman had to be in her early 50's. Now this may sound like I'm exaggerating, but this woman had that "it" factor that made me wonder what it would be like if I explored the possibility of actually stepping to an older woman. As she finished ordering her meal, she gave me the look that said it's ok to speak to me and I won't shoot down your approach if you come correct. She conveniently and casually sat down at the table next to mine and I mustered up enough courage to ready myself to make it do what it do. We began our casual cordial conversations that I hoped would end up giving me a great story to tell, but all hopes of exploring the possibility of aged fine wine were crumbled by the crushing question, "Did you go to school with my daughter?" Absolute buzz killer! Fantasy destroyed, dream diminished and I was back to reality. (good thought though)

Despite the fact the fantasy of frolicking with the fifties plus females failed, I couldn't help but wonder how many things would be different in respect to dating because of age? I couldn't come up with a valid answer to this question alone so I had to throw it out to a group of fellas who assisted me. After the great debate and roundtable discussion, we finally came to a general consensus that had some pretty valid points. Older women know who they are and have a pretty good since of purpose. They're established in their career and aren't out to prove their worth or themselves to the world. They've probably been married before so it's not the end of the world and a big push to jump the broom because they're the last one in their group of friends who hasn't yet. Their biological baby clocks aren't ticking like time-bombs and the children they already have are probably grown and out of the house by now. Baby's daddy drama is irrelevant, text messages happen to be inside text books, they're all played out of games, they know how to cook, periods don't come that often or regular anymore (although menopause might be a problem) AND they know how to let a man be a man and have never heard Destiny Child's song "Independent Women!" They've experienced the ups and downs of relationships and know that it's the little moments that make life enjoyable. (whew)

Now I'm not saying I agree with all of the characteristics listed above OR that they apply to all women, but it did sound good while it was rolling. Nevertheless fellas, I wouldn't be doing us any justice if I didn't tell you that the women can easily say the same about us if the shoes were on the other foot. There are some serious corrections we need to man-up and make regarding our approach to relationships. In fact, my veteran is the women who taught me the lesson of integrity. Integrity in its simplest form can be defined as having the courage to do the right thing regardless of who's looking. She was upfront and blunt about what she wanted from a man. She insisted that there was no need for the lies or excuses that normally accompany the birth of new relationships. She provided a sense of history for me that gave me insight about how there are too many games being played, requirements, needs and wants men were falling short of when it comes to how we treat our women; younger or older.

Lesson #2 – Integrity Matters..So Grow up and Get Your

Grown Man On

I recently went home and had an experience that made me pause for a second to have one of those "I remember when moments." I stood in the backyard of the house I grew up in for the first time in years and realized how small the yard actually was. At one point in my life, that yard was my entire world. As I grew older and was allowed to leave the yard, the block became my world. Then there was my neighborhood, my city, state, country and now the world. The yard amazingly looked so small to me now. I couldn't believe how small my frame of thinking had to be in order for those fences to hold me. The truth of the matter was the yard had not changed at all; I did. The space that immersed my imagination and nurtured my youthful ambitions with possibility was now being viewed through the eyes of a man who has seen and experienced several years of growth. As much I wanted to believe it, the reality is that the yard hasn't shrunk, I've grown. I smiled and laughed inside because no matter how far you've traveled, it's always good to remember where you started.

One of my favorite subjects to discuss is change. I love talking about the decisions we make along our journeys in order to become or make something different from what it used to be. Change is the biological order of the universe. The transitions and how you come to those changes however are far more important than the challenges they represent. Truth be told, it's hard for us as individuals to change. We try to resist it in every way. As a human species we somehow seem to want to maintain the status quo and don't want to push ourselves into unfamiliar places. We all have been engaged in those conversations where we find ourselves talking about what would be the perfect age to go back to or if we had it our way, we would stay age (you fill in the blank) forever. We often find ourselves becoming comfortable with the familiar even if it keeps us from achieving greater success by selectively approaching or doing things differently.

Let me suggest to you that change is the conduit that catapults us into our true purpose. Its equivalent to growth and growth is the natural order of life. Everything on this planet is growing. If something is not growing, it is either artificially made or dead. So my question to you is, "Are you growing?" Have you taken the necessary steps to abandon the spaces, places, people or situations you've become so familiar and comfortable with in order to grow into who you're purposed to be? Are you growing or are you stagnant, standing still and stuck on stupid because of the fears you have of venturing into the unfamiliar?

As men, we're wired to take risk and fortunately you cannot mention the word change without mentioning chance. Take the chance to change and do something different than what you've been doing. Growing is being a grown man and moving out of your parent's house. Growing is not being a womanizer and bragging about how many you have on your roster. Growing is getting a real job and stop ducking the child support system. Growing is having the ability to stop lying, cheating, blaming, neglecting, being irresponsible, irrational and irritated about how you think everybody and the world still owes you a favor! Grow up!

After you've made the decision to grow up, you'll realize that you have to grow through some growing pains that will make you feel a little more uncomfortable than what you're accustomed to. Of course you'll have moments of denial, blaming, anger, confusion, resistance and lack of focus, but you can conquer the challenge of those sentiments by trusting God and the changes you're growing through are making you stronger. Having the boldness and audacity to modify old behaviors places you in a position of greatness. Once you've conquered the challenge of growing through, the only thing left to do is grow on with the newfound life of no longer playing small because of your fears to change. We've all come from different experiences that helped mold us into the men we are today. Staying in the same place with the same people and same mentality is unnatural and isn't what God intended for us. We were born for greatness! I encourage you all to examine your situations, circumstances and relationships closely and make the conscious decision to push yourself to make a change and grow. The world is a lot bigger than the backyard basketball courts we grew up loving and the only way to see and experience that is to accept the challenge of change, take some chances that challenge you to grow up, grow through and grow on.

My Veteran Tracy schooled me like no other woman I'd ever been with. She knew I was younger, hurt and going through my healing process, but informed me that regardless of your rationale and reasoning for not treating women the way you're supposed to treat them, it's time out for excuses and time to start exuding the eclectic essential elements of being good and doing good by women. I learned that it shouldn't take for you to reach your 50s before you grow up and learn how to be real men to real women. She taught me that it's nothing wrong with getting back to chivalry, back to romance, back to communication, compromise and sacrifice. She inspired me to resurrect the resilience that resonated my natural God-given potential to be a man. True, a level of maturity does come with age, but there are some qualities and characteristics that can be easily manifested if we as men learn how to just man-up and stop living out our boyhood dreams. Stop playing games, spending money you don't have on grown up toys you don't need. Be responsible, respectful and righteous. Be honest, humble and have integrity. It's time to get your grown man on! Is older better? I can't really answer that one, but I do know if you trust God and become the man He says you already are, the characteristics and qualities adored and admonished by most women will shine through you regardless of your age. My veteran reassured me that I have the power to shun away the stereotypical suggestions of not being mature and having it together. "You don't have to be older to get your grown man on - - - you just have to be willing to stop making excuses, accept the challenge and make it happen!"

If nothing more, my veteran brought me back to the reality of the consequences of my actions. Experience is a necessity when it comes to explaining and exploring your level of integrity. I needed that in my life and on my team to help me move forward in a positive direction. I can say with no reservations that there definitely need to be more Tracy's out there to help a lot of men snap out of it and grow up in many respects! Thank you Tracy for helping me understand the difference between boys and men.

COACHES EVALUATION SHEET:

Define who you think you'd select as your Veteran player and list the qualities you like most about her?
My Veteran Player is _____
The qualities and characteristics I like most about her are:

1. _____
2. _____
3. _____
4. _____
5. _____
6. _____
7. _____
8. _____
9. _____
10. _____

The lesson(s) I'm learning or learned from _____
is: _____

_____
_____
_____
_____
_____
_____
_____
_____
_____
_____

CHAPTER SIX

THE SUPERSTAR – MY HUMAN HIGHLIGHT REEL"

"The whisper of your ego tends to scream loudly."

Oh we've all seen them and we've all experienced them as well. The superstar is the showstopper. The game comes natural to them and they fortunately don't have to work hard to be who they are. Their amazing to watch and you find yourself often watching and marveling in their magnificence versus playing your role as coach. You either love them or hate them depending on what side of the game you're on. The superstar can write her own ticket. She has every quality and characteristic you can dream and value in a player; she's ideal. Just looking at how well she does what she does is dangerous. They look and act the part so well without you telling them how it sometimes scares you. Superstars are good and they know it. In fact, the very presence of their talent breeds competition from every angle. There will be several other coaches and players elevating their game in an effort to garner her attention because superstars aren't just good, but they make other coaches, players and teams look good also. Superstars are the ones who really don't need to show up to tryouts because you know they already made your roster before they even dribble a ball.

Lesson #3 - Swallow Your Pride & Lose Your Ego

I could walk into a crowed room with her and all the men would try their best to not look. I was halfway through my healing process when I met Candace. She was nothing short of amazing. She was the type of woman that fit all of the qualities, characteristics and criteria I thought I wanted in a woman. In fact, she was very similar to my ex. It seemed as if I found a Candace no matter what phase of my life I was in. I was drawn to them like moths to flames. There were no mistakes about it, Candace represented the very idea of marriage to me. She was giving, nurturing, sophisticated, sassy, self-sufficient, intelligent, funny, had no kids, real hair, didn't need make-up and was finer than the average with an asset that made you say, "Can you tell yo mama I said thank you!"

Candace was my kryptonite because she had the potential to make me weak and not stick to the healing process I'd so wonderfully began to craft. Fortunately,

I met Candace right in the middle of my process. By then I was honest, humble and had an extreme level of integrity to tell her exactly how I felt and where I was in my life. Unfortunately, kryptonite doesn't listen to the truth as you tell it. Kryptonite is more dangerous than alcohol when you're talking about unveiling a person's truth. Because Candace knew we were compatible, comfortable and convenient for each other, she realized it was only a matter of time before she convinced me to give in to the challenge of winning her over. She saw the glimmer in my eyes when I watched her from afar, she saw me fighting my internal urges to want to please her, she even saw me metaphorically drink a gallon of water in an attempt to swallow my pride and not try to one-up the competition when they tried to recruit her. Yep, she had my number and could write her own ticket if I wasn't careful.

Candace was the superstar on my team who was confident, full of charisma and character. In addition, her superstar status came fully equipped with an ego package that gave her access to cripple, cater to and convince me to give in to her every desire. Despite her ability to make me weak and superstar status, whether she wanted to or not, Candace taught me the lesson of how to swallow my pride and not give in to the whisper of my ever present ego.

What Makes Me Go With My Ego?

We've all had women in our lives we've given superstar status to before right? What is it inside of our minds that consistently catapult us into those kryptonic compromising positions? Why is there a constant negotiation process ensuing despite our cognitive ability to decipher between right and wrong? We know she's dangerous and seems to be the same woman we keep falling for, but we don't have the courage, boldness or audacity to say no to her. Ah, the "I" factor; that which feels, acts and thinks of nothing more than self. We've all heard it before and deal with it on a daily basis. We use dirty words like vanity, conceit, arrogance, cockiness and selfish to describe it. Ultimately, it only boils down to one word that consists of three little letters; "ego."

I'll be the first to admit I have a weakness for women and Lord knows my ego has gotten me into more, "What was I thinking?!" moments than I can count! But truthfully, because of our egos, we all have pressure points and things we willingly subject ourselves to that have disproportionate degrees of negative outcomes. We owe our egos for arguments, angers, frustrations, fights, disappointments, dispositions, competitions, regrets and so on. Ego softly whispers and tells us it's ok to cheat because we'll never get caught. It tells us we know the answers to questions over our head, we can win when we've already lost and need to move on. It tells us we're bigger than we really are, smoother, smarter and better. Ego tells us to trust the unstable, inconsistent, insecure, selfish subconscious thoughts we try to manifest into reality.

Ego has everything to do with your subconscious desire to maintain or gain control of a situation, circumstance and/or person including yourself. When we learn to succumb and surrender to the vices of control that hold us hostage, we'll then be able to free ourselves by letting go of the false illusions we perceive as our reality. This endeavor doesn't come without work and sacrifice. Swallowing your pride and losing your ego however will give you a better chance to fight yourself in spite of yourself.

Fellas, it's time for us to be bigger men who choose not to succumb to the whispers and suggestions of our ever present egos. It's time to stop trying to impress people with what we don't have. Stop trying to be someone we're not and start being ourselves. Stop trying to live out or rehash our incomplete boyhood ambitions. Deflate our pride filled chests. Surrender our illusions of control, trust God and not our egos to guide our actions. Be courageous and confident enough to not conform and side with the societal pressures attributed to the defunct definitions of manhood. We're bigger than that, stronger than that, smoother, smarter and ultimately better than something as small as a three letter word right? Of course we are. In fact, today, I vow to go where I want to go and choose not to listen to my ego, but pleeeease pray I don't run into another 5 foot 5, brown skin superstar woman with a pretty brown round and a killer walk before midnight because all bets may be off! (just kidding) Seriously, you truly do have the power to challenge yourself daily to take the chance and make the change of letting go of your egos. Remember, have the courage to surrender, the confidence not to succumb to pressure and the conviction to believe and trust God will transform your egotistical anxieties into righteous honorable actions. You choose what and who your kryptonite is which gives you power over every situation. Learn to let go of that ego man!

Candace was good for me and definitely necessary to help me identify the lack of courage I had when it came to not surrendering to the control of my ego. Superstars are must haves on your team because without them getting to the championship is a long hard road. A superstar is someone you can compare everyone else to. She's your ideal player that naturally has what others have to work hard for. You find yourself weak for her because you know the team would be less competitive without her presence. She's a constant reminder of the potential everyone else can have if they just watch and aspire to be more like her. Forget about the fact that she's kryptonite to you and your process sometimes. Everybody has weaknesses. Superman's was kryptonite. Yours is your Superstar type woman.

Yes, she comes well equipped with a huge ego that wants to be the center of attention. Yes, she is selfish, self-centered and sells the philosophy of "me, me, me" all the time, but she's the superstar and that's how and what superstars do. Are they trouble and a hand full to deal with? "Yes." Just remember to not be too weak, follow through with the team building process and don't give in to her every desire before you're whole enough to handle the potential relationship she can offer!

COACHES EVALUATION SHEET:

Define who you think you'd select as your Superstar player and list the qualities you like most about her?

My Superstar is _____

The qualities and characteristics I like most about her are:

1. _____
2. _____
3. _____
4. _____
5. _____
6. _____
7. _____
8. _____
9. _____
10. _____

The lesson(s) I'm learning or learned from _____

is: _____

_____

_____

_____

_____

_____

_____

_____

_____

_____

_____

CHAPTER SEVEN

WHO'S GOT POINT

*"If you can't stand your own reflection,
how can you expect anyone else to?"*

This position is probably the most important job on the team. The point guard is usually the person who pulls the team together when they lose focus. She leads, guides and facilitates direction. Whoever runs the point has to understand and be able to make spontaneous decisions on the floor as if they were the coach themselves. Coaches depend heavily on them to be the single point of contact on the floor when it comes to communicating and carry out their marching orders. For this reason, it's natural for most point guards to often know the coach's thought processes and sometimes remind and report to the coach what's worked and what's not working. She's usually the player on the team that speaks up the most because the coach listens to her most when it comes to executing game-time strategy. Very smart, articulate and has a spectacular talent for visualizing the unseen, talking bluntly about unmentionables and helping the coach formulate the indecisive actions he's hesitant to take.

Note: This is a meaty chapter and it's crucial that you comprehend the concepts presented in order to make it to the end of your process.

Lesson #4 – Real Men Have the Courage to Tell the Truth

Have you ever had that person in your life that just knows way too much about you and the way you operate? They like the same foods, have the same passions, same zodiac signs, crack the same type of jokes and often even finishes your sentences before you do. If you truly assess them and their personality characteristics, you'll discover that they have the same overall habits, attitudes, beliefs and expectations as you. This woman is so much like you that it's almost like talking to yourself at times. Well meet my point guard Jackie.

Jackie was phenomenal in several ways. She had vision like no other woman I'd been with. I mean she really got me when I didn't get myself. I'd tell her a fragment of what I was thinking and she could break it down into what I was really trying to communicate. Now I was pretty good at bs'ing, but Jackie saw through everything I ever tried to shovel. I told her I didn't enjoy the spotlight and she told me I was made for it and to stop fighting it. I told her I was fully healed from my divorce and she told me how I wasn't quite there yet. I told her I could abstain from sex and she told me how it would be impossible when my weakness was women! Man this stuff went on all the time. I tried my best to not divulge what I was thinking when I was around her, but somehow she'd read my mind every time. I was almost convinced she was a Jedi from Star Wars who used her Jedi powers when she was around me. We'd be sitting around watching TV when a commercial came on with ice cream in it. I'd say, "That looks good, but I don't need it." She'd then wave her hand across my face and say, "You want some ice cream." And I'd change my mind and tell her to grab her coat and let's go get some ice cream. Oh she was good. The truth was I really had a taste for ice cream that night, but I just didn't want to go through the hassle of getting dressed and driving to go get it.

Jackie taught me more about acknowledging the truth about myself than any other woman I met. I considered her to be a genuine reflection of myself; my mirror actually. While I was with her, she taught me to ask the hard questions like what were the things I didn't like about myself, what was I hiding from and what was my purpose in life? She then challenged me to take the steps necessary to correct those faults in order to fully live the truth of who I am. Simply put, Jackie taught me the courage and importance of communication. Speaking up and speaking out about how I truly felt was a lesson I very much needed to learn.

So Tell Me What You Don't Like About Yourself

Unfortunately, Jackie's lesson is one that many of us as men need to learn. We have a problem with expressing our feelings and sometimes get stuck in our own perpetual existence of bad habits. Now I'm not going to say that your vise or hang-up is similar to mine, but we all have something that our mirror reflects. So my question to you now is, "Have 'you' ever asked yourself what it is you don't like about yourself?" Our lives' are so busy and we get so accustomed to our routines that we forget to reassess our original goals and truths. Furthermore, we often find ourselves letting other people dictate and determine the outcomes of our successes. If you truly value yourself, your time and your purpose why are you allowing external circumstances, situations or people to govern and navigate your life? Throughout history, peer pressure has proven to influence more impromptu personal decisions than I can list. Pressure itself is the undeniable paradigm shifter. There only two things an individual can do when pressure is presented in some perspective of their life; you either "focus or fold." Focusing means having the drive, determination, character and courage to confront and conquer whatever circumstance or situation exist. Folding means not having the will, desire or courage to tackle your dilemma and in turn you give up and run away. The problem is that when it comes to self-examinations that entail the pressure of making internal commitments that will help you rectify whatever it is you don't like about yourself, many people would rather fold versus focus.

Fellas, it's time for us to stop running from and focus on whatever we deem the ugly truths about ourselves. It's up to you to make the choice to wake up, look yourself in the mirror and make a serious assessment of where you are and decide what it's going to take to change whatever disposition that has been detouring your destiny. The mirror is an extremely powerful object that allows us to see ourselves as the world sees us. Furthermore, by acknowledging our flaws, faults and fictitious fronts it allows us to redefine, repurpose and reposition ourselves by sculpting graphic depictions of becoming the men God has destined us to be. You know what insecurities, idiosyncrasies and individualized ignorance's you possess. Identify them, develop effective strategies to neutralize them and implement those strategies daily. Telling yourself and anyone else what you don't like about yourself is a very humbling and honest experience. Stop thinking the situation you are in cannot and will not get any better. If you are open to change and a little work, anything is possible. Stop talking about trying to do it. Point out your focus areas of opportunity, develop measurable strategies and make it happen. It's time for you to stand up and become what you believe God for. If you can't be honest with yourself, then the life you're living is a lie! It's time to stop hiding from yourself and unveil your truths.

EXERCISE 1:

Begin this exercise by sitting in front of a mirror where you can descriptively and honestly make a listing of how you view yourself. (Internally & Externally)

I really don't like the following things about myself:

_____

_____

_____

_____

_____

_____

_____

_____

_____

_____

_____

_____

_____

Read this list thoroughly and reiterate to yourself the importance of trying not to become or live out these characteristics. While we're taught to focus on our weaknesses, this list is representative of the ugly you who is open to growth and in no way do you need to focus all of your energy and efforts towards the above.

EXERCISE 2:

I absolutely like the following things about myself:

_____

_____

_____

_____

_____

_____

_____

_____

_____

_____

_____

_____

_____

_____

_____

_____

_____

Read this list, learn it and live it! This person makes you happy and keeps a smile on your face. These are the characteristics that highlight you at your best. Maximize and magnify them 10 times over! Focus the majority of your energy and efforts on finding creative ways to capitalize on these strengths.

Not Even Makeup Can Mask Your Make-up

When I was younger I used to love to play the game of hide and go seek. I was good at it. I used to pick the most unlikely places that people would think to look for me to hide. I can remember countless times when the person designated to seek would become frustrated with their search and cry out, "ok I give up you win!" I would jump out of my hiding spot with joy and satisfaction because my cleverness had prevailed and I had won the game. Nonetheless, despite my competitive nature and ability to win at this game I can remember distinctly having feelings of sometimes wanting whoever was playing the role of the seeker to find me. Not because I wanted to lose, but simply because sometimes it was fun to be found. It kept everyone at a level playing field and interested in the game. You can make a strong comparison to the game of hide and go seek to life itself. All of us at some point in life find ourselves hiding from certain situations, circumstances or people. Moreover, we often find ourselves hiding from ourselves hoping that our true selves will never have to be unveiled. So we wear masks that manipulate the masses into believing the little lies that hide the ugly truths of who we really are underneath and inside. All the while, the quiet cries inside of us are yelling out, "I'm over here" hoping to be found by someone. Someone who agrees, identifies, understands or just flat out gets us. Unfortunately, our desperate attempt to be understood keeps us hiding behind guises of guilt. We wear these masks because they give us a chance to move in and out of character without anyone discovering who we truly are. Despite being cunning, clever and having the ability to execute keen tactics of camouflaging, it is evident that many of us suffer from internalized pains that paralyze our plight, potential, passion and purpose.

The true measure of a person comes from God and from within. Throughout childhood to adolescent phases and even as adults, we often ask ourselves two probing questions, "Who am I and what is my purpose?" All too often those questions are carried as baggage into every facet of our lives. We blatantly bewilder ourselves by blind folding our countless casualties and walking them into our individual messes. In every relationship no matter what the type, we all suffer from problems of the past, dilemmas we never discuss and hiding monsters under the multiple masks we wear everyday. The lack of consideration to communicate our deepest fears and flaws are what helped cultivate the callus culture in which we all coexist. Everyone seems to have a hidden agenda that never surfaces until after comfort levels have been breached and it's too late to back away from that person you could label as the "masked avenger's" life.

So do you know who you are and what your purpose is? Do you truly know or are you just comfortable with masquerading and playing make-believe? Are you parading around full of pride, full of ego, perfect outfit, car, house and public representative persona? If you take it all off will your self-esteem match the mask that you wear daily? Who you are is not determined by what you look like, what you have or your economic status. You are a child of God whose make-up is a direct result of your God given purpose. Furthermore, your make-up proves to be a combination of components that reflect your individual habits, attitudes, beliefs and expectations.

Have you ever wondered why solitary confinement is considered by most to be one of the worst punishments given to a prisoner? I used to believe that it was not as bad as they made it seem. The fact that they do not receive the same amounts of food, water or time outside are all valid reasons as to why solitary confinement can be so bad, but they are not the biggest. Solitary is bad because it gives a person nothing but time to be alone with himself. The stripped down, naked, raw and uncut version of yourself can be terrifying for most. Imagine that, no masks, no vises, distractions or external expectations, just you and God alone. So now you have an opportunity to confront, address and wrestle with all of your deepest fears, flaws, desires and disappointments. All the while, there is no one there to interrupt or stop you from coming to grips with you. Can you imagine the type of conversation you would have with God if you did not have any distractions? The things you would ask Him to take, forgive or give would be extremely life altering.

Similar to solitary confinement, the major problem in life is that most of us are held hostage by the ever present illusions of our public personas. Life is meant to be free, but so many of us are stuck standing still and stagnant in the prisons of our own minds. I understand clearly now what Ernest Campbell meant when he wrote the book, "Locked in a Room Full of Open Doors." That is the position where we often find ourselves as we continue to masks ourselves from our true reality. Locked in rooms full of open doors of opportunity is where we sit while the silence and solitude systematically severs our will, sanctions and seduces us to submit to the habits, attitudes, beliefs and expectations of the mass majority. Unfortunately, the tragedy of tradition is the constant conditioning of mass deception. In order to shift the paradigm an individual has to agree to no longer be victimized, compromised or sympathize with the repercussions and ramifications for rebelling against the ideologies of the majority. Mentally he can then consider himself to be free from the blatantly biased boxes of social purgatory.

The truth of unveiling myself was given to me by my articulate, intelligent and Jedi-mind-trick playing point guard Jackie. Understanding more about yourself, what you think and who you truly want to become is probably the most important step in your process of positioning yourself for commitment. Reflections are the essence of who you are, but can be altered if you do the work necessary to make it happen. If a Jackie hasn't found you in your lifetime, I encourage you to find her in order to help you reveal what you don't like about yourself, unveil your true self and define or reposition your purpose.

This is the most important position on your team and you need to explore and experience what she has to offer you. So the question is, "Who's got point on your squad?"

COACHES EVALUATION SHEET:

Define who you think you'd select as your Point Guard
and list the qualities you like most about her?

My Point Guard is _____

The qualities and characteristics I like most about her
are:

    1. _____

    2. _____

    3. _____

    4. _____

    5. _____

    6. _____

    7. _____

    8. _____

    9. _____

   10. _____

The lesson(s) I'm learning or learned from _____

is: _____

_____

_____

_____

_____

_____

_____

_____

_____

_____

_____

CHAPTER EIGHT

THE ALL AROUND ATHLETE

"Listen twice before you speak."

The last position on your starting five is the athlete. She undeniably has a natural ability to play almost any position. The athlete isn't the most eloquent when they do what they do, but they get the job done. Their jump shot is awkward, but effective. Their defense is average, but consistent. Comprehension of the game is commendable and their level of intensity regularly outweighs their teammates. Truthfully, the athlete is the jack of all trades. (no pun intended) Whatever position you tell them to play, they're available, ready and willing to make it happen because they're well rounded, full of energy and have an unconditional love for the game. When you watch them play, you can't help but remember the early days when you used to be as unpolished as them.

Lesson #5 – Learning to Listen

You're on the last leg of your process and the athlete is truthfully a representation of your entire process. She is the epitome of life's full circle philosophy. Meet my forward Rhonda. Rhonda was the woman who let me know that I had reached a point in my life where I could use the demise of my situation to help others move forward. She was me at the beginning stages of my process of repositioning myself. Every feeling, thought, action or sentiment I experienced as a result of the demise of my marriage, she was undergoing as she was undergoing her divorce herself. She gave me the gift of hind sight, but I couldn't fully experience that without first learning how to truly listen.

I was watching the Oprah show one day (I know…I lose some man points for that, but bare with me) and something very interesting caught my attention. Apparently, Oprah has a new reality show called the "Big Give" and had the winner of its first season on to share and celebrate his experience. The incident that stood out the most was when Oprah asked the winner to describe his most memorable moment on the show. The winner then reflects back to a moment where he volunteered to help in a soup kitchen. It was there when after serving food he also decided to help wash dishes and had an opportunity to spend some time with a young guy who opened up and shared his hard knock life story with him. The pivotal point in the story was when the winner of the game out of the kindness of his heart asked the guy, "What can I do to help you?" The guy replied confidently and humbly, "Nothing." He then went on to further say, "I just appreciate the fact that you *listened* to my story and hopefully you can pass it on to help someone else get through their situations."

I think all of us can identify with the above story to a certain degree. As men, we have an inherent ability pre-wired into our brains to want to help solve or fix whatever situation or circumstance presented to us. We're problem solvers by nature and its hard for us to feel like there's nothing we can do to help rationalize, rectify and resolve a problem. Unfortunately, sometimes there's nothing to do, but truly listen to whatever message a person is trying to convey. As the old folks say, "God gave us two ears and one mouth so we can listen twice before we speak."

The art of listening is very hard to do because you have so many distractions or noises surrounding you. People can be in the same room listening to the exact same person and walk away with two totally different messages. How does that happen? Well, as humans we act in accordance to the truth as we believe it to be. We dissect whatever someone is saying to us into little pieces of personal puzzles. We then put all of the pieces back together for our own purposes. Truly listening and being able to clearly understand what a person is trying to communicate to you requires a sacrifice of your self.

You have to clear your mind from all of the internal and external distractions that dissipate and dilute your ability to ascertain and understand the necessary from the noise. Simply put, learn to turn the "you volume" down. It's not always about what you can do to save the day or how you can help resolve the issue. Try to focus on the messenger behind the messages you receive and remove yourself totally from the equation.

There are so many folks who simply need and want a listening ear. There are folks who have been crying and screaming inside for someone to truly take the time to see them, hear them and make a genuine connection to identify with them and their given situation. The homeless person holding the sign you ignore, the old man who moves and talks to slow, your woman who expresses her most intimate feelings, the child pulling on your pants leg while you're on the phone, the needy friend, troubled teenager, crazy co-worker, nosy neighbor, WHOEVER! If we learn to pause long enough to take ourselves out the equation and truly listen without judging, justifying or jumping in as the hero who saves the day, we'll be able to make more meaningful connections to folks who deserve the acknowledgement and confirmation that they do matter and they aren't invisible.

Fellas, learning how to effectively listen takes personal discipline, compromise and sacrifice. Moreover, you'd be amazed at how the simple act of truly listening to someone impacts change in a person's life. We get so consumed with our own agendas that we sometimes forget that the simple things in life often mean the most. Spend time instead of spending money, giving of your self instead of giving gifts and learning to listen instead of leading the tireless drive of trying to be the hero and saving the day. God gave us two ears and one mouth not by accident, but so we can truly make a connection with others by listening to whatever is pressing upon their hearts and minds. If you haven't tried it, I encourage you to make a point to do so. Your life and someone else's will definitely be blessed by the simple act of listening.

Rhonda captivated my attention and I listened to her with an open heart and mind. I remember how I used to be so quick to try to have all the answers, but with her, it was like listening to my self talk to my self. She needed someone who understood and could relate to her situation more than ever at that point in her life and I did just that. By truly listening to her, I unveiled some truths about myself that I'd been pushing off throughout my entire process. My road to relationship readiness had been harder than I remembered and she instrumentally reminded me of that by teaching me to truly connect with someone by listening and learning from their story.

Lesson #6 – The Best Form of Giving is Forgiving

Teaching Rhonda how to cycle through her anger, disappointment, discouragement and disillusions strengthened my level of confidence in the possible fruition of future relationships being a success. There was one piece missing from my process and if not for Rhonda I'm not sure I would have made it to the end. Rhonda taught me the lesson of how the best form of giving is forgiving. Learning how to forgive all of the hurts, hard times and headaches that were a result of your last relationship was the missing link I'd yet to discover for truly moving on and becoming whole enough to be fully committed to another woman. Through listening and counseling Rhonda, I reminded myself about the need to forgive who hurt you and more importantly the need to forgive myself for holding onto the pain, anger and disappointment of what transpired for so long.

Does She Really Need to Know Everything?

Now this wasn't my situation, but I think you'll understand where I'm coming from better if I articulate my point with the below scenario. I facilitate a relationship recovery group specifically for black men who have suffered from broken relationships and have a desire to move past some of the hurts they've suffered as a result of their demise. Now I know the first thing most of you are thinking is that there's no way you'd subject yourself to sitting in a room with other grown men talking about how she was the only love of your life. Trust me, I wouldn't either. Fortunately, that's not the premise of the program I offer.

For example, one of my most recent groups had a very interesting true to life discussion about forgiveness and the process it takes for a man to truly reach the point of surrendering his fear of coming clean. Hypothetically, let's say in your mind you've messed up and done some things in the context of your relationship well beyond the realm of reconciliation. The relationship you once knew is now over due to some he said she said drama. You know she has a good suspicion of how fowl you really were throughout the relationship, but nothing was ever proven or said by her. You also know deep down inside how you've wronged her over the years. You've lied about being at work when you were really with your woman on the side. You've stolen money from the account for the child you never told her about and blamed it on the bank. You repeatedly made promises only to break them over and over again. You only tolerated her parents, never said anything about her cousin hitting on you, the other phone you've had for 2 years, so called business trips out of town and so on. You've spent some time apart and you now realize that she is your one and only true love and you want her back in your life. You also know because of the unanswered suspicions you need to begin with a clean slate, but then think to yourself,

"My bag of dirt is so heavy there's absolutely no way she'd even think about accepting what I deem to be a sincere apology if I was up front and told her the truth, the whole truth and nothing but the truth!" "How could she possibly ever forgive me?"

Forgiveness is a very tough subject to tackle because it's received different by everyone. Some people have a humbling spirit and can easily forgive someone for not doing right by them. On the other hand our grandparents taught all of us how women know how to forgive, but they surely don't forget. With that weighing heavily in the back of our minds, how much truth do you need to reveal? Does she really need to know everything? I mean, what she doesn't know won't hurt her right? Besides, I'm a changed man now and the past should just stay in the past. She should be more focused on our future and how good I plan on being to her now and not worry about the "old" me. (you really do deserve a hand clap for that speech) Spoken so eloquently, but unfortunately, that's not exactly the right approach.

If you truly wanted to be with this woman and truly want to start over, you have to start by first forgiving yourself and then allowing her an opportunity to forgive you as well. If you carry the baggage of your dirt around long enough, eventually the bag will spring a leak and some of that dirt is going to spill out for everyone to see. Trust me, the side piece who you stopped calling because you "changed" will somehow get your new address and perhaps stop by to check in on the happy family. The child's mother you never told her about will run low on funds and decide to file for child support. The cousin who tried to talk to you will flip the script and say you tried to talk to her. Your woman will find an old cell phone bill, etc, etc.

Fellas, there's an old saying about how the truth will set you free. When reconciling any type of relationship, forgiveness is a precursor to receiving that freedom. We often try to subconsciously trick ourselves into believing our wrongs will somehow dissipate and disappear if we keep them to ourselves; they won't. We'll always have the feelings of guilt and paranoia due to the fear of the secrets we carry being discovered. Forgiveness and full disclosure is your freedom. Go to the person and share your side and reveal the facts as you see them. Unfortunately, you're at the mercy of the other person, but it's your duty to put it all on the table and give them a chance to decide to restore the relationship. As you look back, you hate what you did and the pain it brought to the lives' of you and your family. In fact, you wished it never happened, but because you've grown and faced the fear of fully disclosing your ugly truths, you can take pride in not carrying the burden of guilt and paranoia everywhere you go and into every new relationship you build. Challenge yourself to trust God enough to know if the relationship is in His will, the forgiveness necessary for it to move past the hurtful truth will definitely happen. And oh yeah, before you decide to tell her "everything" make sure there's nothing around she can grab that will do you bodily harm! Forgiveness is freedom.

Now I'm not saying this scenario applies to you or my self. I simply wanted to show you how forgiveness plays out when the shoe is on the other foot. What I am suggesting is for us as men to better learn how to forgive others for the wrongs they've inflicted upon us. The longer we hold onto and carry the baggage of those past pains around, the harder it is trying to commit yourself to another woman because you're thinking she's either going to do the same thing to you or you find yourself holding back parts of you that need to be unveiled, but you're too scared to do it due to what happened in the past.

I could see that truth clearly in myself as I got to know Rhonda each day. She was broken and struggled to find the fragments that pieced together her puzzle of life. Believe it or not, Rhonda is a coach's dream player. She isn't wet behind the ears, not old enough to be on her last leg, doesn't have an overwhelming ego and doesn't think she knows more than the coach. Rhonda is what most coaches refer to as "coachable." She has all of the necessary components to be a great basketball player, but they aren't overbearing like everyone else's on the team. Her humility, honesty, integrity, pride less, non egotistical, courageous forgiving spirit propels her to the top of any coach's list of favorites. After all, she's an all around player that possesses a little bit of a lot. Without Rhonda, my process would have failed miserably. She was definitely the missing link that helped catapult me into the category of committing myself to a healthy lasting relationship again. The best form of giving is truly learning how to forgive. Not just the people who've hurt you, but learning how to forgive yourself as well.

COACHES EVALUATION SHEET:

Define who you think you'd select as your Athlete and list the qualities you like most about her?

My Athlete is _____

The qualities and characteristics I like most about her are:

1. _____
2. _____
3. _____
4. _____
5. _____
6. _____
7. _____
8. _____
9. _____
10. _____

The lesson(s) I'm learning or learned from _____

is: _____

_____

_____

_____

_____

_____

_____

_____

_____

_____

_____

THE SECRET WEAPON – THE 6TH MAN OFF THE BENCH

*"Habits help determine your future so
be careful which ones you keep"*

Now the 6th man off the bench is the wild card. This is the player who's willing to do anything and everything to earn a starting position. She goes hard whenever she's called on. In her book there's no substitute for sacrifice. She dives for loose balls, gives hard fowls, plays aggressive defense and stays after practice late to perfect her game. She's going to leave it all on the floor every night in hopes that the coach notices her valiant efforts and decides to replace one of the starters who is showing some slack in their game. The 6th man enters the game when one of the starters needs a breather or isn't doing their job to the coach's liking. She provides a burst of energy, excitement and fresh air to the game for however long she gets to play. Her overall purpose is to win the coach's approval and her motto is "go hard or go home." The 6th man is every starter's nightmare because they know she's waiting in the wing without remorse to take their position.

Lesson #7 – Resisting the Urge to Substitute

Your team is complete and you really don't need any additional players on your roster, but the secret 6th man off the bench somehow creeps onto your list. Although you knew you only needed 5 players to play, you still have your eye on this special player. Don't act dumbfounded because I'm talking about this. We all know who our 6th man off the bench is very well. She's the girl who we can call when we need some extra attention, affection or affirmation about who we are. She validates and satisfies the wild side of us and should in no way be considered non threatening. Allow me to introduce you to Keisha. Now I'm not going to say much about Keisha because I might need her assistance in a time of trouble if you know what I mean. However, I will say this. We all have a Keisha somewhere on our roster and I think it's imperative you understand why her presence is so prominent. Keisha makes us feel good about ourselves whenever our self-esteem or ego is bruised. Simply put, Keisha is our failsafe device when self-destructive situations arise. She eases our nerves, brings us back down to earth and well...she rocks our world until we forget about all of the problems we thought we had. Of course what's problematic is that Keisha tends to show up regardless if we're in a relationship or not. She's trying to earn a spot on your team and knows how to get your attention and knows your weakness very well. Actually, she's the most dangerous player on your roster. So what is it that keeps us from saying no to the Keishas of our world?

It's Just Something About Her

So you two have a love hate relationship. Truthfully, there's more hate than there's love. You can't stand her outlook on life, the way she treats her kids, the annoying small talk, why you argue every time you see each other, her short haircut, know-it-all mentality, quick temper and that overbearing perfume she drowns herself in. She's been fading in and out of your life for years. You really don't see or talk to each other often, but when you do, you pick up where you last left off. You know she's toxic and also there's no way you'll ever be together. You try to get rid of this woman almost every time you see her, but can't shake her. When someone asks you what keeps you going back, you find yourself shaking your head, looking into space with wrinkles on your forehead saying, "It's just something about her."

Now we've all had at least one of these in our lifetimes and probably just got a chill after thinking about them now! You could be in a relationship, have two kids, a house and a dog named Oliver, but when you get that call from her, your insides have that exciting tingling sensation. She claims she wants to see you and "just talk." You know what she wants and although it goes against where you are in your life, you give in like you always do. What is it about this woman you just can't resist? What type of spell has she cast on you? You really don't like her and know she's bad news, but in a twisted way you can't get enough of her.

Now most of you would say it's the sex. She got that "comeback" right? Ok, personally I'd agree with you to a certain extent because in my day I've had some...(clearing my throat) Nevertheless, I'd professionally tell you that it's not just the sexual escapades or the indescribable something about "her" that keeps you two connected; it's something about "you." Tough pill to swallow I know, but the truth hurts sometimes. Relationships are nothing more than cognitive conscious connections with people, places or things we choose to maintain. Our habits, attitudes, beliefs and expectations are a result of the decisions we choose to undertake on a daily basis. The woman you can't shake has become a habit for you. You've formulated an attitude of acceptance about her presence in your life. You've convinced yourself to believe there's no way you can resist her regardless of the repercussions or ramifications associated. Therefore, the expectations you set for yourself are to submit to her call for comfort, conversation, company and countless compromising positions of pleasure-filled moments! (sigh) Simply put, she's not the problem, you are.

As men, we have an undeniable connection to our egos and pride. That's why she can talk about you for being whipped, call you a punk and everything else in the book and you rush to her ridiculousness to prove her wrong. Our pride and egos get us into trouble every time. We know it's wrong, we know she's wrong for us and we really have nothing in common, but we keep stringing the relationship out because of our inability to be courageous enough to say no. No to our egotistical, pride-filled, lustful, childish, catch-a-girl-get-a-girl attitudes that keep us attached to the strings of those toxic relationships we know ain't good for us!

Fellas, life is about the choices and decisions we make which ultimately determine our direction. Although the temptation of the one you can't let go seems hard to reject or resist, it's possible if you trust God and don't succumb to the subtle suggestions of your ever-present ego. I know it's difficult, I've been there, but I also know it can be done. There's something inside of you telling you, "its ok." It's not. Learn to step outside of yourself, view and think about the hurt, harm and damage being done to both of you as a result of this ongoing relationship. This isn't about her making the decision to cut the cords of convenience that keep you connected, you need to make it happen. So the next time she sends that late night text or calls with the need to just want to talk, be man enough to resist the temptation and stand by your decision to know its not about resisting her, it's about being disciplined enough to resist yourself.

Why Can't Men Stop Cheating?

Ok just in case it hasn't soaked in for you yet, here's another scenario I think will help you better understand the psychology behind cheating. There was an email circulating around the internet earlier this year entitled, "Why I cheat on my wife." Believe it or not, I've received and I'm still receiving this email from multiple women requesting I write something on the topic of why men cheat. (sigh) Here's the short version recap for those who have never seen or heard about the email in question. This guy claims he loves his wife, loves his kids and his life, but since he's a man, he can't stop himself from wanting other women who aren't his wife. In his words, *"there's a part of me that just can't handle monogamy."* He doesn't want to have sex with every woman he sees, but from time to time he has strong sensations and urges to be with other women; and oh yeah, he happens to act on those urges. He then attempts to give valid reasons why he does what he does. (sigh again)

Here's the thing, unfortunately, everyone has a different individualized perspective on this topic and trying to address it on a broad generalized scale is border line suicidal! However, from a counseling perspective, if you truly dissected this guy's point of view it's easy to ascertain the levels of insecurity, ego and lack of purpose that exists. Unfortunately, the truth of the matter is that these levels and characteristics tend to exist in several men and women. We're all human and most people tend to respond better to circumstances or situations they're confronted with based on how the situation or someone makes them feel. In example, if I'm married, *"feel"* sexually neglected and not fulfilled by my spouse and sex is extremely important to me, I'm going to be more easily persuaded by my co-worker Keisha's suggestive flirtations about how she'd promise to drop it like it's hot on a regular basis if she had a man like me in her life. I'd listen more closely to how she can't understand women who stop putting out once they get married. Now normally, I wouldn't pay her any attention, but since I'm *"feeling"* punished and deprived by my significant other for an argument that didn't go her way, Keisha is close, available and ready to make me *"feel"* good by satisfying my animalistic urge to release my roar. Is it right for me to act on that urge? Not exactly, but as humans we have a natural tendency to act in accordance to the truth as we believe it to be. Our perceived reality becomes our reality because we find ourselves reacting to impulses of affirming our human need to emotionally stabilize what's become unbalanced.

Without all of the psychological babbling, life boils down to choices. Despite the presence of pressure, any degree of deprivation or the absence of feelings of any sort, God still gave us the power to choose. So often we want to push the blame onto other fictitious factions of our faults, failures or shortcomings we forget that our dilemma began with the simple word called "choice." Why do some men cheat? Simply put – insecurity, ego and/or greed. Some of us tend to be so insecure with who we are or the situation and circumstance we're in and because of the overcompensating presence of our ego, we want to make ourselves feel better about ourselves by allowing someone other than who we're currently with to feed and build our egos up. Now the question then becomes, "Isn't one woman enough to handle that?" This is where greed plays its pivotal role. If the level of insecurity is that low and the ego is that high, the numbers increase on how many it takes to stroke the ego back to feeling secure. Furthermore, society puts so much pressure on us to define ourselves through relationships we fail to do the necessary work it takes to be honest enough to first explore and define ourselves as a whole person before becoming a part of someone else's life.

Fellas, despite the stereotypical view of all of us being cheaters, I know there are several good, honorable and righteous brothers who know how to not succumb to their insecurities, egos or greediness. And for the fellas who happen to struggle with cheating, learn how to surrender you sensations to the courage of conquering yourself. Learn to fight yourself in spite of yourself. Life is about the choices we make daily. With that said, you cannot say choices without mentioning chances. Chance involves risks. Take the chance to make the hard choice of challenging yourself to change your self- destructive behaviors. Truly take the time to discover who you are and who God purposed you to be. And as for the guy in the email who really never should have gotten married in the first place - - man to man - - I'd tell him to grow up, get real with himself and stop killing his soul and his family's soul softly!

Keisha or whoever your 6th man off the bench is should be considered dangerous, but you have the power to choose whether or not you want to play her or even add her to your roster at any time. You're the coach man! Relationships are hard enough and don't need any added headaches associated. Learn how to not succumb to your insecurities, egos or greed and the Keishas of the world won't be a problem for you during the long haul.

Coaches Evaluation Sheet:

Define who you think you'd select as your 6th Man and list the qualities you like most about her?

My 6th Man is _____

The qualities and characteristics I like most about her are:

1. _____
2. _____
3. _____
4. _____
5. _____
6. _____
7. _____
8. _____
9. _____
10. _____

The lesson(s) I'm learning or learned from _____
is: _____

_____
_____
_____
_____
_____
_____
_____
_____
_____
_____

CHAPTER TEN

WHO GOT NEXT...
I'M READY TO PLAY!

So now you've made it to the end. The goal of rebuilding your team is complete and you're probably wondering, "So what does it all mean?" Life is a process and understanding the lessons given to us over the course of that process is essential to our growth as men. When it comes to expressing our deepest sentiments, explaining our points of view or sharing our stories women can run circles around us hands down. Fortunately, that has nothing to do with our levels of comprehension. We live by the rule keep it simple. We don't need all of the superficial circumstantial conversations that always end with, "I wish you'd just talk to me." We get it, it's just harder for us to express what's on our mind if we aren't really sure about the subject. Sure we can b.s. our way through a few tight spots, but being confident in what you're talking about plays a lot smoother. With that said, I hope now you're more confident in understanding and expressing the motives of why you do what you do, connect to certain women and the components that comprise your character.

Relationships are hard work and require you to give your full undivided attention to discovering the components that comprise the character you convey. Although we utilized the building a team analogy throughout this book, the secrets to becoming who you're purposed to be already exist inside of you. By analyzing the relationships you've been exposed to, understanding the lessons learned as a result of those exposures, choosing the right woman for you and committing yourself to healthy lasting relationship should no longer be a huge issue. Despite the fact I used the analogy of the starting five of a basketball team, in no way does it take five women for you to become whole. Sure variety is nice and I understand playing the field, but again I stress that all of the components you need to be whole and happy already exist within you. This was my story and way of letting you know why and what the majority of us get from multiple encounters with women. Your relationship story and lessons you've learned over the years may be totally different and that's ok. You don't need an entire team to teach you all the lessons I learned. Truthfully, you can get it all from one person if you're lucky. Whatever the case, remember you have the power to challenge yourself to become who God has purposed you to be. Regardless of the pitfalls that leave us feeling powerless and in peril, continue to have the boldness, audacity and courage to discover all of the components that make you whole and who you are. Until then you'll always be searching for something bigger and better.

Settling down is hard, but by better understanding yourself and why you do some of the things you do, I pray your road to experiencing happiness and success as it pertains to a relationship works well. Which type of woman you choose depends on your taste and what turns you on the most. If you like young and inexperienced then pick the 1st round draft pick. If you like older and experienced then the veteran is definitely the choice for you. Your idea dream girl is the superstar, your twin in a skirt is the point guard or the all around coachable type is the athlete. Uhhh... and forget about it fellas, the 6th man is not an option! There's no right or wrong answers here, you hold the key to unlock the doors of opportunity. Regardless of what type of woman you choose from your relationship roster, if you take the lessons of honesty, humility, integrity, courage, communication, swallowing your pride, losing your ego, forgiving and resisting the urge to cheat, I'm certain that you're destined for happiness. God bless you and much success in your self-discovery process and choosing the right woman once you're whole enough, available and ready to make it happen.

"Keep the faith, keep making it happen and remember to stay out of your own way!"

Jack A. Daniels

COACHES PLAYBOOK

Pre-Season Analysis Questionnaire

As discussed throughout this book, being ready for a healthy lasting relationship is about being comfortable and content with you being whole as a person. When you consider yourself to be a whole person and can live your life happily without relying on another person for your happiness, you might be ready to commit. In essence, you're ready to be in a relationship when you come to the consensus that you don't need a relationship.

1. Do you currently have a desire to be in a committed relationship?
    a. Strongly
    b. Mildly
    c. Maybe someday
    d. Are you crazy?! I don't know if I can do it!

2. When do you think you'll be ready for a committed relationship?
   a. Right now
   b. Give me another year or two
   c. 5 years
   d. I'll know when the right one comes along
   e. I have no idea
   f. When hell freezes over!

Do you have valid reasons for wanting to be in a committed relationship? What are they?

_____

_____

_____

_____

_____

_____

_____

_____

_____

_____

_____

Coaches Playbook on *Fear*

Now that you've read my story, what are the fears keeping you from settling down and committing? (List up to four)

a. _____

_____

b. _____

_____

c. _____

_____

d. _____

_____

Go back to those 4 things and grade them on a scale of 1 to 10 (with 1 being least fearful and 10 being most fearful) How valid are (were) those fears? Did you have good reason to be afraid?

a. _____

_____

b. _____

_____

c. _____

_____

d. _____

_____

Action Plan:

What action will you take to confront and conquer your fears?_____

_____

_____

_____

_____

When will you be ready to make this happen? List a target start date/time below.

_____

_____

_____

_____

Coaches Playbook on *Mistakes*

What are the stupid mistakes you make that you need to correct or watch out for throughout your process? (List up to four)

a. _____

_____

b. _____

_____

c. _____

_____

d. _____

_____

Go back to those 4 things and grade them on a scale of 1 to 10 (with 1 being the least and 10 being the most) How valid are (were) those mistakes? Did you have good reasons for making those mistakes?

a. _____

_____

b. _____

_____

c. _____

d. _____
_____

Action Plan:

What can you do to improve in each of these areas? How can you make it less likely that you would make these mistakes again? Find one action step you can do in the next month to improve where you're falling short. (Note that this step will probably not get rid of the problem totally, but it should make things somewhat better)

_____
_____
_____
_____
_____
_____
_____

Name one friend who might encourage you to follow through on these steps. List his/her name and when you can ask that person for help.

_____

Coaches Playbook on Values

After reviewing your life and the relationships you've encountered, what qualities & values do you want most in the woman you choose?

(a list of values is on the next page)
List of Values:

_____

_____

_____

_____

_____

_____

_____

_____

_____

_____

If you lived in a perfect world, could you mold your perfect woman from this list?_____
After reviewing all of the lessons you've learned from the relationships you've had, what characteristics and values have you discovered most about yourself?

_____

_____

_____

_____

_____

_____

_____

List of Values

Abundance	Consistency	Fame	Kindness	Rationality
Acceptance	Contentment	Family	Knowledge	Recognition
Accountability	Content over fluff	Fidelity	Leadership	Relationships
Accomplishment	Continuity	Flexibility	Learning	Reliability
Accuracy	Continuous Improvement	Flow	Liberty	Religion
Achievement	Contribution	Focus	Logic	Resourcefulness
Acknowledgement	Control	Forgiveness	Longevity	Respect
Adaptability	Conviction	Fortitude	Love	Responsibility
Adventure	Convincing	Freedom	Loyalty	Righteousness
Affection	Cooperation	Friendship	Love	Risk-Taking
Aggressiveness	Courage	Frugality	Making a difference	Romance
Agility	Courtesy	Fun	Mastery	Safety
Alertness	Creativity	Generosity	Maturity	Security
Ambition	Curiosity	Giving	Meaning	Selflessness
Anticipation	Daring	Going the Extra Mile	Merit	Self-esteem
Appreciation	Decisiveness	Goodness	Mindfulness	Seriousness
Assertiveness	Delight	Grace	Modesty	Service
Attentiveness	Dependability	Gratitude	Money	Simplicity
Audacity	Desire	Growth	Motivation	Sincerity
Awareness	Determination	Guidance	Non-violence	Skill
Balance	Devotion	Happiness	Openness	Speed
Beauty	Dignity	Harmony	Opportunity	Spirit
Belonging	Diligence	Hard Work	Optimism	Stability
Blissfulness	Discipline	Health	Order	Strength
Boldness	Discovery	Helpfulness	Organization	Style
Bravery	Discretion	Heroism	Originality	Systemization
Brilliance	Diversity	Holiness	Outcome Orientation	Teamwork
Calm	Drive	Honesty	Outstanding Service	Timeliness
Candor	Duty	Honor	Passion	Tolerance

Carefulness	Eagerness	Hopefulness	Peace	Tradition
Caring	Education	Hospitality	Perceptiveness	Tranquility
Certainty	Effectiveness	Humility	Perseverance	Trust
Challenge	Efficiency	Humor	Persistence	Truth
Change	Elation	Imagination	Personal Growth	Unity
Charity	Elegance	Independence	Pleasure	Variety
Cheerfulness	Empathy	Influence	Poise	Well-Being
Clarity	Encouragement	Ingenuity	Positive Attitude	Wisdom
Cleanliness	Endurance	Inner Peace	Power	
Collaboration	Energy	Innovation	Practicality	
Comfort	Enjoyment	Insightfulness	Precision	
Commitment	Enthusiasm	Inspiration	Preparedness	
Communication	Equality	Integrity	Presence	
Community	Excellence	Intelligence	Preservation	
Compassion	Excitement	Intensity	Privacy	
Competence	Experience	Intimacy	Proactivity	
Competition	Expertise	Intuitiveness	Progress	
Concentration	Exploration	Inventiveness	Prosperity	
Confidence	Expressiveness	Investing	Punctuality	
Connection	Fairness	Joy	Quality	
Consciousness	Faith	Justice	Quiet	

Coaches Playbook for Relationship Readiness
When you reach the point of relationship readiness
(which may be another 3 – 18 months down the
road) what do you think your life will look like? In
5 to 10 sentences, describe yourself and how you'll
look in the future. What will be different about you
between then and now?

_____

_____

_____

_____

_____

_____

_____

_____

_____

_____

_____

_____

_____

_____

_____

_____

_____

_____

_____

_____

ABOUT THE AUTHOR

Jack A. Daniels has an eclectic background of professional counseling, entrepreneurship, teaching and corporate leadership, that provides a unique perspective and approach to educating, enlightening and empowering people to move forward and maximize their potential.

He is the founder and President of the life changing non-profit personal growth & development organization 'Press Pause.' www.press-pause.com He is also a Nationally Syndicated Columnist, writing a weekly column printed in multiple newspapers, magazines and internet blogs entitled, *'For the Fellas'* that focuses on the passions, potential & plights of Black men. (over 2 million readers worldwide) In the past, several critics have labeled him as the "Men's Relationship Resource."

Be on the look out for his upcoming book releases entitled, "I Need a Wife…Where are the Real Black Women?" and his highly anticipated book entitled, "The Power of the Pause." Residing in St. Louis, MO, Jack continues to be a conduit and catalyst for impacting, instituting and initiating change in multiple respects. He has been and continues to be nationally recognized for his tireless efforts, focus, innovation and passionate work within the Black community.

For more information and bookings please go to www.press-pause.com or send emails to info@press-pause.com

Printed in the United States
133965LV00001B/6/P